Silence Is Premeditated: A Collection
By
Amy Laprade

Acknowledgements:

I wish to thank all who've contributed to this project:

Paul Richmond, Kathy Dunn, Donald Fisher, Geoffrey Blüh, Albie Park, Stuart Mieher, Todd Walker, Roxanne Bogart, Kevin Cook, Pamela Sneed and the Solo Performance Class of Sarah Lawrence College, Stephen O'Connor, Jonathan Mirin.

I would especially like to thank *Plum Literary Journal* for publishing "Silence" and "Irresistible," May 2017 edition, and *Write Angles Journal* for publishing "It Can Only Be Seen In Darkness," and "The Invitation" for the December 2017 and June 2018 editions, and *Silkworm* for publishing "Air and Amnesia" in the *Silkworm 11*: the Eleventh Hour Edition, October 2018, and *Meat For Tea*: the Valley Review for publishing "No Women In Pink Spandex," Volume 12, Issue 4, Ginseng, December 2018.

This book is dedicated to family,
Jack and to Geoffrey Alexander Blüh.

Published by Human Error Publishing
www.humanerrorpublishing.com
paul@humanerrorpublishing.com

Copyright © 2019
by
Human Error Publishing
&
Amy Laprade

All Rights Reserved

ISBN#: 978-0-9991985-7-5

Cover design
by
Paul Richmond and Amy Laprade.

Portrait photo by Paul Richmond

Images by Amy Laprade.

Human Error Publishing asks that no part of this publication be reproduced or transmitted in any form or by any means electronic or mechanical, including photocopy, recording or information storage or retrieval system without permission in writing from Amy Laprade and Human Error Publishing. The reasons for this are to help support publisher and the artist.

Table of Contents

Air and Amnesia	11
Silence	13
United We Stand	19
White	23
The Invitation	27
Irresistible	31
The Scribbles Aileen Makes	37
Faulty	41
An Old House Never Sleeps	43
Sunday Morning	45
It Can Only Be Seen In Darkness	47
In Slow Motion	51
Suburbia	55
1405 Van Ness	59
Dreams of Stardom, Donna Summer, and God's Kingdom	67
No Redheads In Pink Spandex	71

Air And Amnesia

there are no boardwalks
no bridges

only one step at a time

arms to the sides
will not offer balance

forget what they told you.

There is only the net
and it is full of holes

and the pool
is packed with concrete

a pitchfork
curves toward the sky
like a smug grin
under the leaf pile.

Don't jump
fall
glance over your shoulder
or down below

there is nothing to see

air and amnesia
blank paper and broken plates
licked clean of memory

there is only existence

you
waiting to be born.

Silence

is a series of dots
that never converge
an elliptical cadence
of a conversation dropped
due to a bad connection.

Speech impediments run in families.
We stutter our apologies.
Always, we say, I'm sorry
but never really mean it.

Silence is the understudy for such platitudes.

The things we want to say
but can't
means that it is all in our heads.

Second guessing ourselves
is an automatic safety feature for our mouths

no hazard shall arise from
having not said
what we can't take back

means having too much to lose
and too much at stake

is the inability to speak on command
therefore
forever holding our peace
of mind
lost...

is the ability to sit on command
to bark only when called.
It means "good doggy."

****

Silence does as it pleases.
It never checks in
and always assumes no
really means go.

It is the sound of
a dial tone
a slamming door
a key turning in the lock

It is
a shrug
walking away
waiting for others to step in

It is decidedly not my problem.

A grunt
a huff
an eye roll
an inaudible sound of an inward sigh

this too is silence.

****

Silence is the sound
of elevator music
on a crisis hotline...

...I am left on hold
for so long
I hang up.

Silence swaggers in with a smile
after a long spell of sadness

giving away possessions
they are better off without
me
when I say goodbye without warning.

Silence is leaping into the sky
and never coming down
concealing a bad habit
and a deadly weapon.

****

Silence is violence
dried in the creases of your knuckles when you
promise me it won't happen again.

It is the lull between a clap of thunder and the
power going out

the dawn creeping under our blinds after a very
long night.

The silence that follows means I meant everything I said

with a seasick fluttering in my chest, fireworks
going off in my head, the gun going off in my
dream.

Silence is premeditated.

Me saying, "I'm fine," even as I sob,
you responding with "That's nice"
when you ask me how my day went, is silence.

is radioactive waste
buried many miles under the ground.

~

Silence is something we do
when we have no words to describe
why we do what we do.

It is a smokescreen
an elephant performing tricks
to make us laugh

the clown inside us all
who fills our heads with caramel corn
and cotton candy
to hide our fears and keep us distracted

the bystander inside us
who wants no part of it

the gas-lighter inside us
who insists that the sun rises in the west
sets in the east

Silence is a certain style of breathing

Sucking it up
and holding it in

never letting it out
or letting it show

all alone together

we subsist on spoonfuls of air

even as we suffocate.

United We Stand

If you're oxidizing,
turning rancid from within
take a step back
and look again.

If you're dosing
yourself to sleep
take a deep breath
learn to cry again.

Do not judge
the feeling of empty
just be
walk with it a while.

Take in the sounds
the sights, the smells
the feelings
and the whys.

Because shooting from the hip
means looking no further
than the end of your finger
pointed at the neighbor
whose name you don't remember.

Do not stuff your feelings,
drown your sour with the taste of sweet.
Obesity is not a retirement plan.

Buying new items
won't bring new ideas.
Shopping is a form of sleeping.

Do not rant
in front of a screen,
then complain you
have no voice.

It takes half the time
to shout, "I'm angry
confused and scared!"
to a warm, breathing body
with ears and a heart.

Do not sink
to the bottom of a bottle
bottom of a vial,
burn yourself to the filter.

Do not shoot up
shoot yourself
shoot your children

To escape
we must exit full screen.

Learn to love again
laugh again
be human again.

Don't be perfect
just be decent

even when we disagree.

Learn to trust
at the risk of getting burned.

Come together again
root for ourselves again
united we stand.

White

Like a wet suit
skin-tight, impossible to strip off.
History unable to peel free from itself.

The chafing between my thighs
not bad—at first.
But after many miles
many years, rubbed raw
movement becomes impossible.
The burning becomes bleeding.

You've bled your whole life.

But I offer no "I'm sorries."
Apologies are cliche
and never make a dent anyway.

Until the day comes
when I truly mean it
when my actions match my words,
the best thing for me to say is

nothing at all

holds more iron
more gravity than

I'm sorry

is like saying "Yes, but the Irish were treated terribly too,"
or arguing that *all* lives matter

me, dropping a quarter in the jar
for every time I've had to explain
the ignorance of my words.

I offer no guilt
because doing so

would mean I am more sorry
for my own discomfort
in this wet suit
that chafes me each day.
Guilt seldom learns from its mistakes
seldom finds a way
to do better going forward.

Guilt is for those
too busy defending themselves
to listen to what yesterday
is trying to teach us about today.

The Invitation

"You seem like you
could use a friend,"
he told her. "You
know, you could
hang here...you
know, if you like
to party...you could
cut school and uh
I got cold beer. And
I could turn you on
to some reefer."
His eyes stroked
her pale thighs,
spilling below the frayed
hems of her denim shorts.

She'd turned thirteen
and it was a year
for busting out.
Her clothes
from last summer
no longer fit. Neither
did her attitude at home.
How to belong
to the in-crowd at school
was a mystery to her
and she wasn't sure she
cared enough to try.

Busting out. Boys. Freedom.

Cutting school, eh?
Needing a friend, eh?

His eyes
the color of rain
turned to sleet,
slick and hard

like panes of glass.

She looked away
at the ground
at the packed dirt
overrun with crabgrass

He held his gaze
from the cracked concrete stoop,
his Harley parked
under the willow
that shielded
the pink, paint-peeled
house from the baking heat.

The half moons
on the window shutters
made her think of
half-lidded eyes.

She folded her arms
cupped her elbows
shifted her weight from one foot
to the other wondering
where his girl Maxine was.

She'd never not seen Maxine around.
The two were inseparable
their leather, their boots
his long hair
her fabulous fashion sense
inseparable.

Except Maxine was gone
along with her ear
for listening to adolescent woes
whenever Mother wouldn't…
and here he was
and far too old.

"Umm, thanks
but I have homework."
She mounted her bike
and his eyes were felt
all the way down the street
as she peddled away.

Irresistible

Cool like the Virginia waterfalls
his eyes undressed her
and yet his stiff smile
demanded such reverence.

Rust-gold
like the hawkweeds of summer
his eyelashes cast fringed shadows
on his cheeks
whenever he closed his eyes...
freckles floating
like nutmeg
on his creamed complexion.

His touch
caused the downy ringlets
on her neck
to stand rigid, the way
static electricity did
whenever they came
together.

His ownership of her
confused her since
ownership of anything was
something she'd never understood
never having owned anything herself

material wealth
ties
an identity.

Her ownership of him
lasted all of one hour
each day of each week
months stretching into years
or however long it took
semen rivulets

to carve shame
into his flaccid
forty-year-old flesh

to erode history
from the face
of Mount Rushmore,
that stiff smile
still commanding such reverence

while
she lay prone
her face forming
an indentation
in the shape
of a question mark
on his pillow, blood
on satin sheets
leaving a period
on the end of a lifelong sentence.

~

When she was eight
her petticoat had been
spattered red with rage
fueled by displacement
blurred boundaries
and lost lineages.

He'd taught her not to cry
no matter how deep the wound
handkerchief pressed to her temple.

He'd taught her everything
she knew about life
everything: plants, animals, music, culture.

She'd learned to tie her own shoes
to smile

and keep going.

This, she'd learned
with a pat on the head
his hands, the color of powdered wigs
soft like the feather of a quill pen.

These days'll never end
she'd assumed, wanting
what he'd been to her
what she'd been to him
to remain as it was
always.

~

But her spidery countenance
had begun to plumpen
and curve

to strain
against every seam
of every garment

beauty bursting at all angles
had filled the gaps
of a self-effacing smile
where there'd been baby teeth.

Her siren good looks
had sealed that once
respectable distance
between master and minion
where the ragged edges of adolescence
once reigned

when one day
while serving tea
her supple silhouette splashed
upon the sunlit floor

of his chamber
her eyes
green-flecked pools
of liquid amber shimmering
in the fading light
gave way to buttons popped
his smooth, soap-like hands
unlacing the ribbons
on the fine gowns he bought her

Irresistible

she was
and he was
all she had
would ever have.

Confusion
over this new way
in which he regarded her
drove her to please
to hold on in the confusing way
she knew how

and though
her actions said yes
she felt certain
she meant to tell him
no.

The Scribbles Aileen Makes

The house is broken
behind all that blooms.
Behind a manicured lawn
where a flag is flown...

where boundaries blur
between brother and sister
sister and Grandpa,
and the scribbles Aileen makes
when she steps out of line.

~

"Her hands never could
keep to themselves,"
you state during an interview.

But then Aileen learned from the best.
Ask Grandpa
the neighbors
and the john johns
that'd come sniffing
in the tall grass
where folks dumped refrigerators
junked cars
and wayward daughters
who gave head
to neighborhood boys
in exchange for dime bags.

Who would admit they knew her?

Did you know her when
she braved bitter frost, in a tent?
Subsisted on dumpster scraps?

Did you know her when
folks trashed her

saying she smelled funny?

Laughed at the rumor
about her being swollen
with her brother's baby?

Did you know her
only when you felt the need,
but then pretended not to see
when she waved
from across the street?

Pretended to be deaf
when she called your name?
Called for help?

Did you know her only
after she made the headlines?

When she gave you fame
for airing her dirty laundry?

"Another blow. Another bag."

You say she's a whore
Perhaps you are the whore

You call her a murderer.
you murdered her,
not pausing to consider
that America birthed a monster
when it failed to serve and protect...

a system broken
behind all that blooms,
behind a manicured lawn
in a small, heartland town
where a flag is flown

a girl broken—broken into

while America bleats about God
country and family values,
and the boundaries blur
between brother and sister
sister and Grandpa

the scribbles Aileen makes
when she steps out of line.

"Faulty"

Naughty gristle
a blind pink animal
nestled among
faded flannel sheets.

"Cheap"

he repeated, his voice
close, vibrating her
eardrum. Stinging
words, a scratched
record, mantra or
some stupid ass slogan.
Inflection dirty
taunting, as if it were
she who'd done wrong.

"Cheap."

he repeated, his muggy
fetid breath sending shivers,
Inflection dirty
taunting, as if she were
a half-this, half-that creature
and faulty somehow.

An Old House Never Sleeps

baby shower pink
shutters winking flirtatiously
at traffic roaring past
the burnt brown yard

paint peeling
like Daytona blisters
on Coppertone bodies

mold blooming below
bulging porch boards
where nature has metastasized
and snakes slumber soundlessly
among squirrel skeletons.

Sunday Morning

Curtains
gather and release
in hushed, rolling waves
rise and fall like lungs
exhaling the scent
of thawing mud

Robins
bounce furtively
between puddles
under the rusty swing set,
excavating slippery pink threads
from Earth's fabric,
damp and matted
like the hair of a newborn
in the lemon light of day

The last snowbank
clutches the ground
like a scab on a slow healing wound
in the shadow of the north gable

A lazy, uneven drone fills the air
the plane, a tiny white dot
skims the vast blue ceiling,
its contrail leaving a scratch

The stutter and thwack
of basketballs on blacktop
curses and grunts
a game gone wrong
broken by the trill
of the downstairs piano.

It Can Only Be Seen In Darkness

Once, during daylight hours
Niles heard strange noises
inside the walls of the church:
sighing and whistling—not
the sweet, melodic kind but
the perverse kind, followed by
cat-calls and wheezing.

The sounds made his neck muscles
stiffen, his flesh crawl, and his saliva
burn metallic from fear. He ran.

Safely outside, he caught a whiff
of something sour as the rear door
swung shut. He never wanted to step
inside of that church again.

He didn't have a choice.

Tonight, there are burn marks
in the red-carpeted aisle. The
choir books are slick with mucus
pages torn from their spines
like limbs from a paper doll
strewn across the pews' cushions.

Hymns of holy worship
reduced to confetti
the aftermath of an unholy celebration
attended only by an empty nave and chancel.

Hammer in hand, eyes darting about
Niles begins his task when a fuse blows
and he is plunged into darkness.
He hears the noises and looks up.

A creature, the size of a cat
quivers between two pews like

sea-foam in an ocean breeze.
Its iridescence reflects the sky
by moonlight. Its membranous
flesh trembles in the cool draft
bulges and then pops.
Effluvium fills the air.

Niles gags. He thinks about bolting
but the glowing EXIT sign watches him
like a red, angry eye from the rear of the church.

Niles has spent his entire life running:
from a son he'd had with a lover,
from a wife who never forgave him
for an affair he'd had with a girl
half his junior...

...his second wife has fallen ill
from a rare respiratory disease
and the bills are mounting

he'd be fired if he left early again.
The boss didn't care about strange
noises inside of walls.

Niles's heart pounds
as the creature slides
quick and furtive as a Black Racer
toward the altar—it's opossum-like tail
atrophied and dragging, paints wet streaks
on the carpeted aisle. The streaks would later
leave more burn marks.

The creature reemerges from the shadows
illuminated by fingers of moonlight that
seep through the window of stained blue glass.

~

Sensing the man's presence,
as incongruent in this place of worship
as a songbird lighting on a solar flare,
the creature recoils and
flattens itself against the wall
below the framed Mother of Mary.

Imagining the dour look
on his boss's liver-spotted face
and the shunt in his wife's abdomen
Niles gazes at the creature's iridescence
noting his own reflection in its faceless head.

Horrified by what he sees
he raises the hammer.
He brings it down.

In Slow Motion

Doorbell rings. Girl inside the house answers door. Admirer on stoop greets girl. Jealous boyfriend stands beside girl, sees admirer. Jealous boyfriend pulls gun on admirer. Girl sees gun. Girl passes out.

Girl comes to. From the sidewalk, she watches girl inside the house answer door. Girl from the sidewalk watches admirer on stoop greet girl inside the house. Girl on sidewalk watches jealous boyfriend stand beside girl inside the house. Watches jealous boyfriend pull gun on admirer. Girl on the sidewalk watches the girl inside the house pass out. The girl on the sidewalk passes out too.

Girl on the sidewalk comes to. From across the street, she watches girl on the sidewalk watch the girl inside the house, who answers the door. Girl from across the street, watches the girl on the sidewalk, who watches the girl inside the house see the admirer on the stoop. The girl from across the street watches the girl on the sidewalk, who watches the jealous boyfriend stand beside the girl inside the house. The girl from across the street watches the girl on the sidewalk, who watches the jealous boyfriend pull a gun on the admirer. The girl from across the street watches the girl on the sidewalk pass out, watches the girl inside pass out. Girl from across the street passes out too.

Girl from across the street comes to. From a block away, she watches the girl from across the street, who watches the girl on the sidewalk, who watches the girl inside the house answer the door. Girl from a block away watches the girl across the street, who watches the girl on the sidewalk, who watches the girl inside the house observe the admirer on the stoop. The girl from a block away watches the girl from across the street, who watches the girl on the sidewalk watching the jealous boyfriend stand beside the girl inside the house. Each girl watches the jealous boyfriend pull a gun on the admirer. The girl from a block away watches the girl across the street pass out, who watches the girl on the sidewalk pass out, who watches the girl inside the house pass out. Girl from a block away passes out too.

Girl from a block away comes to. From above, looking down, she watches the girl from a block away, who watches the girl from across the street, who watches the girl on the sidewalk, who watches the girl inside the house answer the door. All admire the admirer on the stoop. All observe the jealous boyfriend, standing beside the girl inside the house. All watch the jealous boyfriend pull a gun on the admirer. Girl from above watches the girl from a block away, who watches the girl from across the street, who watches the girl on the sidewalk, who watches the girl inside the house pass out.

Doorbell rings. Girl from inside the house answers door. Admirer on the stoop greets girl. Jealous boyfriend stands beside girl, sees admirer. Jealous boyfriend pulls gun on admirer. Girl from above watches the girl inside the house who sees the gun. Girl from above watches the girl inside the house intervene. Girl from above watches the girl inside the house grab the jealous boyfriend by the arm. Girl from above watches the girl inside the house observe the bullet exiting the gun's chamber in slow motion.

Girl from above watches the girl from a block away, who watches the girl from across the street, who watches the girl on the sidewalk, who watches the girl inside the house observe the bullet moving toward admirer.

Girl from above watches the girl from a block away, who watches the girl from across the street, who watches the girl on the sidewalk, who watches the girl inside the house observe the bullet moving toward admirer in slow motion. All watch the admirer dodge the bullet.

Girl inside the house watches girl on sidewalk get shot, who watches girl across the street get shot, who watches girl one block away get shot, who watches girl above, who watches the girl inside the house get shot. Girl from above passes out.

Girl inside the house comes to. Doorbell rings. Covered in blood, girl from inside the house answers door. Boyfriend on stoop greets girl. Jealous admirer stands next to girl, sees boyfriend. Jealous admirer pulls gun on boyfriend. Girl inside the house, covered in blood, passes out.

Girl inside the house, covered in blood, comes to. From the sidewalk, girl covered in blood sees the girl inside the house, covered in blood, answer the door. The girl from across the street, who is covered in blood, sees the boyfriend on the stoop greet girl, who is covered in blood, inside the house. The girl from a block away, covered in blood, sees the jealous admirer pull a gun on the boyfriend. Girl from above, covered in blood, sees girl inside the house, who sees herself covered in blood, being observed from above.

The girl from above, sees the girl from a block away, who sees the girl from across the street, who sees the girl on the sidewalk, who sees the girl inside the house, who sees herself from above, covered in blood. All heave a sigh of relief when the admirer's gun fires a blank.

Suburbia

Walk lights disrupt the osmosis of traffic, congestion slithering like a torpid snake. Your steps fall into a staccato rhythm to the chirp of the walk lights as you cross North White Plains Road.

Safely on the other side, you pass a one-level brick home, a rotting jack-o-lantern on its stoop and bars over its ground-floor windows. You wonder, is the house under arrest? Or under witness protection? Are the bars there to protect the house from prowlers? Or to protect prowlers from the house? The shades on the windows are drawn. The house is asleep.

In the yard, there is a baby sycamore, branches covered in a synthetic thread-like substance, made to represent spiderwebs. Plastic tarantulas lurk inside them. They are the sycamore's way of scaring off trick-or-treaters, even if it is the first of November.

Autumn's last leaves cling to the sycamore's branches. One very rebellious leaf has held onto its green. It dangles like a trail marker among a sea of orange and gold.

A green leaf in November is neither a miracle nor a fluke. Neither is a dandelion in December. The seasons must work harder with each passing year to keep up with themselves. At 7:08 a.m., it'd been eighty-seven degrees. Now, at 4:30, it is thirty-four degrees. It is as if the month of November suddenly remembers that it is November.

The geese roil above in a broken V, as if struggling to keep up with themselves. They are about to miss their flight. Every year, their vacation destination is the same. Every year, they fly Southwest.

Your pace quickens when you reach the plaza. All that remains of the day is a stratum of clouds, purple and bruised against an atomic sunset.

The street lamps flick on as you cross the lot. Their halogen eyes watch you from above as they bathe you in silver light. You are grateful for this since your friend, Borders, the final building on the edge of the plaza, insists on living in darkness. Your hopes are dashed.

The darkness of Borders is in mock defiance of the other brightly lit storefronts. A warmth radiates from Starbucks—its neighbor, who tries to console you with its Harney and Son's Hot Cinnamon Sunset Tea. You have no use for beautiful things.

You have a morbid fascination with failure. You gravitate toward the defunct, the desolate, the decaying. You have always been this way. You are here to see Borders, once part of a thriving, sprawling community, now deceased. Deadweight clinging to the glory of its big box cousin, Papyrus.

An atrophied appendage. A callous. Dead skin clinging to live, breathing tissue. The corner slice of a thick crust pizza that no one wants—except those with a passion for crust and a love for being cornered. With a name like Borders, the building is inherently crusty and doesn't want to be wanted.

You step into Borders' concrete slash for an entrance. The shadowy crevice envelopes you in darkness and does nothing to shelter you from the biting cold. You peer through the double glass doors but see only the throat of an empty stairwell.

You wander to the side entrance, corralled behind a black, chainlink fence. Tree shadows spread along the building's stucco facade, craggy and irregular like arthritic fingers. The shadows shimmy against the cracked foundation from the force of the wind, which sends leaves scraping along the pavement.

Your fingers ache in the November chill as you clutch the cool, wire mesh, catching a glimpse into the soul of Borders, once teeming with shoppers. Its windows are black, sending a vibe that is both camera-like and watchful. Clouds are reflected on the glass like cataracts floating on the jelly of irises—perhaps sails drifting on the still, high seas.

Vandals from outer space may one day hurtle stones the size of city blocks at the windows. The building's alarm will sound. The glass will await the tsunami, gear itself for impact—feel the shockwaves of a static economy.

The basement windows are lit to discourage vandals in a place where there are no vandals. You wonder, who are the keepers of the light? You wonder if these keepers make daily rounds—shut off the daylights during the light of day. Perhaps daylight savings during a blackout will take on a more meaningful meaning.

The lit up basement makes Borders appear even more desolate. The escalator is frozen in a permanent downward gesture, leading to an empty, bile-colored room that had once housed romance novels and murder mysteries. Square silhouettes on the walls mark the place where paintings once hung—as if the paintings have left their shadows behind.

Chrome faucets jut from the opposite wall, resembling necks of dead geese. Their former use is a mystery to you. The closing of Borders is a mystery to you.

1405 Van Ness

Eugene led Dawn and I down a dim, grey-carpeted corridor reeking of stale cigarettes, old plaster, and other unidentifiable smells. In a sandpaper voice he explained that I'd be sharing the kitchen—a trapezoidal room no larger than a walk-in closet—with two old men. And though it made my last pad—a studio over a garage—seem like the Ritz Carlton, its north-facing window did provide a spectacular view of a Beefeater Gin billboard, which loomed large over a ten-story office building. From the narrow gash of a window, Dawn and I gazed upon a forest of air ducts and waste pipes jutting out from a patchwork of oily rooftops like industrial worms.

The bathroom looked like a psych ward. It had white tiles and a tiny window, caged by iron bars. It had a view of an air shaft that plunged five stories below. In the apartment adjacent from mine, a man stood in his bathroom window. Clad in a terry cloth towel, he whistled an unfamiliar tune while shaving. Coastal breeze wafted through the bars, kissing our skin for the first time since we'd entered that stuffy Victorian-style building, which I suspected had been a hotel at the turn of the century. The numbers still hung over the doors, but were washed over with dingy, off-white paint.

Giddiness percolated in my belly at the idea of living on my own for the first time. Unable to conceal my feelings of uncertainty, however, I looked searchingly at Dawn. She nodded, her dimples exploding as she cracked a grin. It was her way of letting me know I could do it. She looked speculative a second later, however, and her bright, blue eyes darkened as a man lurched into the hallway, clad in just his pajama bottoms and smelling of booze. He peered at us through bloodshot eyes. My skin crawled as I shot him a hard glance.
"Your neighbor, Jim," Eugene grumbled.
Jim grinned. "Afternoon, gals."
Ashamed by my own snootiness, I returned Jim's greeting with a half-smile, my eyes not meeting his. Dawn giggled. At what? I didn't know, but I joined her anyway. Eugene

grunted. Disapproval registered on his shapeless, freckled face at the tattered sleeping bag slung over my shoulder, along with my stinky backpack containing a week's worth of dirty clothes, a clock radio, and diaries which bore my soul in ballpoint ink. He probably had his doubts as to whether I could come up with the four hundred a month that it took to rent this dump in the heart of San Francisco. His keys made a jangling sound as he unlocked the last door on the right.

A single, high-ceilinged room with ample sunlight sprang into view. A radiator hissed and clanged in the corner, even though it was mid-July. I stretched my arms out, greeting the room with a smile. I already had a spot staked out for my sleeping bag. I'd later place it over the mysterious brown stain in the gray carpet, near the closet. Having endured weeks of couch surfing, roach hotels, and noisy dormitories, I ached for my own space.

The previous night, Dawn and I, and a gaggle of travelers from around the world, were lounged on the roof of the European Guest House, passing forties of Mickey's Malt under the stygian sky, where the stars never materialized from under that sheath of ocean mist. The foghorn, moaning beyond the mouth of the bay, and the cheerful but foreign "ding ding" sound of the cable cars clattering up and down Powell and Mason streets, reminded me that I was three thousand miles from home. The stars, slumbering among the scent of Eucalyptus and damp coastal air, fell around me. Their luminosity shattered in my eyes like seashells on the wrangling shore, and flickered like broad daylight. I didn't know much, but I had energy and I had time on my side. I was young and everything and anything was possible.

"Don't fall into the drug scene!" My big sister preached before dropping me off at the Amtrak station less than a month prior.

"Call me collect as soon as you get there." Mom choked back tears.

"The laundry room is in the basement. Be sure to lock the door behind you or homeless people will find their way in." Eugene's lecturing tone cut into my thoughts as my eye followed the earthquake cracks from the ceiling's Victorian trim to the baseboards, bubbling with paint drips, which met the cigarette-burned carpet.

"Downtown is the safest place to be during an earthquake," Zachary, a slacker kid from a rich family in Connecticut, who'd landed a job at the hostel, told me. "Because it's built on bedrock, unlike the Presidio which is built on nothing but landfill. Landfill is the worst. During tremors, it acts like jello. Homes built on it quiver until they collapse. The gas mains bend and burst. That's how the Marina went up in flames during the '89 quake."

Whether Zachary was an authority on earthquakes, or not, was beside the point. His eyes, the color of lapis, and his unruly crown of curls that sprang from his head like fireworks and smelled of papayas, kept me sniffing at his heels for affection. We'd hooked up on my last night at the hostel. He'd be the first in a succession of West Coast heartbreaks. Manipulative Phil, who loved to gamble for a living, and who looked like Chris Robinson of the Black Crows, would be next among this succession.

Toot! Toot! The distant but forlorn sound of a doorman's whistle snatched me from my daydream. I'd later discover that it came from a fancy hotel at the tip of Nob Hill. Its piercing but musical decree would wind its way through the grit of the Tenderloin before reaching my fifth-story window, which overlooked the four-lane traffic of 101.

"You're on your way," Dawn assured me after Eugene had left, over the din of traffic that occasionally rattled my windows.

"Yeah...." I replied non-committal, wishing she could stay longer—realizing that this was it. I had just ten dollars to my name after handing Eugene the cash for my first, last, and deposit. Later, I'd have to hit up a Western Union.

For the last three years Dawn had lived up the road from me. A day didn't pass when we didn't see each other. We'd spent previous summers swimming at the river, getting drunk on cheap wine, and acting wonderfully stupid at parties. We'd spent restless nights driving along rolling country roads with no destination in mind, hoping that 107.3 would play "Come As You Are," that new song by Nirvana. Crickets would thrum in the fields beyond our cracked windows. Often, coffee at a twenty-four-hour truck diner was our entertainment for the evening. What was there for her in Massachusetts?

Dawn shook her head gently without me having to ask the question. I understood then that I had to take this journey alone—that my dreams were not hers. Silence fell between us as daylight faded to dusk.

Sunsets were different on the West Coast than the ones in New England. In California—fog aside—they were golden, cloudless, and uniform. They never varied.

New England sunsets, on the other hand, were like cotton candy filaments, blazing among a sea of purple plums, where fireflies flickered along its shore in June. In August, the sun, fuchsia, fat and swollen, would slump low in the sky. At dusk, its nuclear rays would cast hazy, rose-colored hues on the birch trees. Had I made a mistake?

"I should get going," Dawn said. "Train leaves at ten...."

I nodded.

"Love ya, Ame." That was her nickname for me. We hugged long and hard. "Stay in touch."

And she was gone. And I didn't know when we'd see each other again. And for a moment, I didn't even know where to go from there. I only knew I couldn't...go back. So, I remained in the middle of the empty room for a long time, hearing the traffic and the blare of the TV that came from my other neighbor, who lived on the other side of the wall, whom I had yet to meet. My bikini lay limp among the clothes I'd dumped in the middle of the floor. I shivered. The summers here were cold, and nothing like the balmy ones in Massachusetts. Like the fog, fear began to creep in.

I sat in the window facing East, my skin glowing pink from the neon light of the Ellis Brook's Chevrolet sign, just outside, and watched the sky change from a faded, denim blue, to a deep gold, to a silvery grey. Fog fell in wisps over the rooftops of buildings but hadn't yet blotted out the moon, now a waxing crescent, that rose over the glittering skyline. I admired the panoramic view of the financial district. Like the needle on a compass, the Trans America building jutted triumphantly over the throng of lesser skyscrapers. It'd later become my north star, guiding me wherever in the streets I may wander.

There was a Circuit City across the street, which boasted many windows. Fifty or sixty television sets flickered in the windows, each displaying the same movie: Dances with Wolves. I fell in a trance, watching fifty or sixty Kevin Costners gallop mutely across the Great Plains on a quarter horse while music played softly on my radio. KFOG was San Francisco's rock station and played some of the same classic hits Dawn and I listened to back home.

"...he knew right there he was too far from home...." Bob Seger lamented over the airwaves in "Hollywood Nights," while a cluster of young people staggered out of Bar 101, across the street. The Irish sports dive had a wide-screen TV but no claim to fame except that it served strong drinks. It was already 10:00 and I needed air.

I rode the elevator to the marbled lobby. There, I paused to gaze at myself in the old, beveled mirrors. There was one on each wall. Each mirror created a dozen replicas of myself. Each replica representing the phases I had yet to go through. If I waved, so did the other Amys. If I nodded, the other Amys did too. When I smiled, the other Amys followed suit. All twelve of us made silly faces in the mirror. We kicked one leg high in the air, looking like a row of Vegas show girls. We were gearing up for classes we'd later take at Jean Shelton's School of Acting.

A man, sporting dark shades, startled me as he came barreling through the lobby. I froze. My smile faded, and I suddenly saw a reflection of the back of my head in the mirror behind me. It was like I could see what other people might be seeing when they looked at me. It was unnerving.

The man ignored me as he opened his mailbox. My cheeks blazed hot, nevertheless, as I bounded past him, letting the cool, damp air slap my skin as I pushed the heavy, glass doors open. Outside, the coastal wind was picking up as it often did around this time, and as usual I wasn't dressed warmly enough.

Last night, when I was uncertain as to whether or not I'd secured the room at 1405 Van Ness, I dared myself to venture beyond The Galaxy theater, where the neighborhood stank of urine and teemed with men dressed like ladies, who called me "sugar," and who cruised the corner of Larkin and O'Farrell in hot pants, while smoking Newport menthols. The bums tried to sell me used clothing out of shopping carts. One of them, named Harry, who'd been hanging out in front of a twenty-four-hour donut shop and smelled of pachouli, told me stories about San Francisco during the sixties. He kept pausing to ask me if I had a cigarette, and ten times I had to remind him that I didn't smoke—in the months that followed, that would change, when I ventured deeper and deeper into that stinky neighborhood. Although, I never did see Harry again. San Francisco was like that—transient.

I never found out if Zachary's theories on earthquakes had been correct or not, since the only tremors I'd come to experience in that magical city were of the personal kind, occurring in a series of aftershocks. My soul, having rested on emotional landfill, rocked and swayed during each provocation. I came close to collapsing at one point, but didn't. Life experience had become a kind of retrofitting, and was the very thing that helped me to remain solid and standing.

Dreams of Stardom, Donna Summer, and God's Kingdom

At eight years old I'd idolized Donna Summer and had big dreams of one day becoming a pop diva. However, living in a rural, working-class town among the rolling hills and farms of Western Massachusetts, dotted with white churches and dairy cows, I was miles away from show business and the glitter of the big city. At eight years old I'd sway my non-existent hips to the beat of my scratched-up record. With a potato masher for a microphone, I'd lip-sync Donna's lyrics in my clammy, basement room instead of doing homework. My parents would then yell, "Amy, stop daydreaming."

In third grade I was sore that I got cast as one of the fourteen angels in our school play instead of landing the part of Gretel, in *Hansel and Gretel*. Bored by my bit part, I spaced out and forgot my cue while imagining myself starring in a motion picture. The teacher yelled, "Amy, pay attention!"

Dancing and singing lessons were out of the question. My parents didn't have money for such frivolities. Dad worked six days a week, even working the graveyard shift at the Boston and Maine Railroad to make ends meet. Church choir was my one outlet for developing my singing and stage presence. It also made Sunday school bearable.

I dreaded Sunday school, not because I didn't want to pledge my allegiance to the bearded man in the sky but because sitting on those hard church pews that were as ancient as the mummies of Egypt and stank of mildew and mothballs, was torment. So was loving Sheila, the mean girl with buck teeth who always kicked me on the playground, because Steve the pastor, in his booming, velvety baritone, was always reminding me that God wants us to be good to our enemies.

Sunday school also meant getting hollered at by Mom for wearing white tights with grass stains on the knees to church. Why would God care about grass stains when I was missing my morning cartoons for him? Well, okay, maybe the stains did have evil connotations. After all they were green like the Wicked Witch of the West, or like the unwanted green potato chips left at the bottom of the StateLine potato chip bag. Green chips were rumored to be poisonous. You might die if you ate enough of them.

At eight I was already terrified and fascinated by death and wanted to secure myself a spot in God's kingdom among the fluffy clouds. This produced conflict, however, since I wanted Heaven and God's love but I also wanted to be like Donna Summer, who sang steamy lyrics like "Dim all the lights sweet darling cause tonight it's all the way!" Not that I understood what those lyrics meant. Church choir was an opportunity for me to obtain salvation and talent—until I grew bored during practice.

"Your voice is flat," Laurie, my big sister, moaned in my ear. "And you always come in at the wrong time because you're always daydreaming. That's why Julie won't give you a solo."

I couldn't help it. My attention always strayed on Lois, who accompanied the choir on the upright piano and wore glasses with lenses as thick as a telescope's. She must've been one-hundred years old and would outlive us all. Her arthritic, liver-spotted hands would fly furiously across the keys as we rocked that wood-paneled, white-washed colonial church, singing "Rise and shine and give God to glory, glory!" The rickety old pews would creak and sway as we'd stamp and sing-shout the lyrics to "Noah's Ark."

While clapping to the beat, I managed to count the abundance of Lois's moles of various shapes and sizes. Rust-brown and fleshy, they cropped up everywhere on the back of her neck and made me think of toadstools in an enchanted forest after a summer rain. Dad would smack me if he were here to see me staring at this woman so rudely. I couldn't help it. Like death, Lois both fascinated and terrified me. I was terrified by her age. I wondered then if that would one day be me. I wanted to ask, "Lois, are you afraid to die? Did you too have dreams of becoming a pop diva? Did everyone yell at you to pay attention and to stop daydreaming?"

But I knew I wouldn't be able to frame these questions for her in the way that they'd entered my mind in that moment. After all, I was just eight years old, and at eight years old I couldn't articulate my fear, lurking like the spiders under the dock at my grandparents' summer camp—fear that the big people—adults—always tried to make small, because my head was too little to take on such big matters—which was another thing they were always on me about—thinking too much about big matters. As far as they were concerned, I had no business inquiring about old age or death before I could get a handle on how to ride my bike without getting my bellbottoms caught in the spokes or taking a spill in the dirt driveway.

How could I approach Lois with my questions when I couldn't understand why I sometimes felt like crying when I saw Donna perched atop of an old-style radio on the, *On The Radio* album cover, sporting a tight floral dress, her silk heels casually dangling from her feet in a seductive manner. Was I destined to go straight from being eight years old, with a nose too big for my face and a nervous squeaky voice that sounded perpetually flat, to being eighty-plus years old? Was I destined to bypass blossoming into that twenty-something year old with a voice like a crystal flute that brought diamond tears to the eyes of even the most cynical of adults? What if I went from gawky to arthritic? From singing on the potato masher in a dank basement, to playing the upright in a musty church? Gee, Los Angeles seemed far away....

I resolved to eat the green potato chips at the bottom of the StateLine bag in hopes of not quite dying from them, but perhaps becoming so ill I'd fall short of my death bed. Maybe then Mom and Dad would feel bad and give me the singing lessons. "Oh, Amy, stop being so dramatic!" they'd say.

"Amy," Laurie hissed, her cold fingers pinching me under my choir robe, startled me, and I glanced around. The song was over and everyone else was seated but me, including Lois, who dabbed at the sweat on her forehead with a hanky, a small smile of satisfaction curled on her rubberlike lips. Perhaps the church choir was as good as it was going to get for me.

No Redheads in Pink Spandex

Earl Gray was fixing himself lunch when the door at the end of the hall slammed, followed by THUMP, SHUFFLE SHUFFLE. THUMP, SHUFFLE SHUFFLE. Beatrice's six-foot frame filled the kitchen archway. Her foot was cocooned inside a plaster cast that vaguely resembled a wasp's nest. She'd busted her ankle chasing two Jehovah's Witnesses from her stoop.

Not much frightened Earl. Only Mama, who had died when he was twenty—and Beatrice when she was furious. With a build like a potbelly stove Earl was not a wispy man, but Beatrice towered him by five inches.

"Last time I'm gonna tell you. No redheads in pink spandex hanging around my stoop at 3:00 a.m.!" Beatrice boomed.

"But…." Earl's voice rose to a plaintive pitch. His eyes grew dark like Brach's black licorice Jelly Beans. "But Boss Lady—"

"Tut-tut!" She wagged a finger. "I am managing an apartment building, not a bordello. My name is Beatrice Buttrick, not the Crown Heights Madame."

"But Boss Lady, I can't live without…." Earl scratched his salt and pepper stubble, his eyes meeting the water stain on the ceiling as he struggled to remember. "Cassidy…? Billy Jean…?"

"So many you can't keep track of 'em! They ain't your girlfriends! Girlfriends don't date guys old enough to be their grand pap! And they don't wear pink spandex leggings!" Beatrice snarled, hands perched on her ample hips.

"Brenda. Name's Brenda…."

"Tenants are complaining. Fannie told me that Miss Betty…"

"Brenda."

"…laid on the buzzer, waking her from a dead sleep. She came out to the kitchen and overheard you two going at it: "Ooh, Earl. Ooh, Earl. Ooh, ooh, Earl! Who wants to listen to that after they've worked a double?"

"She's my girlfriend."

"Don't you lie to me, Earl. You don't think I know who goes in and out of my building? I've seen Miss Betty…"

"Brenda."

"…on several occasions. Ain't tellin' you again. No redheads in pink spandex. No kit-kat girls on my property."

"Fannie Dungworth's a liar and a klepto. She drank my two-liter bottle of Hillbilly Holler…oh, and a box of Cosmic Brownies went missing from my dresser. She's been picking my lock. I know this cuz I put a quarter on the red tile in front of my door." Earl thrusted a sausage-like finger at the red and white-checked floor. "When I came back, the quarter was on the white square."

"Oh, Earl…" Beatrice groaned, placing a weary hand on her forehead.

"Fannie used the last square of toilet paper and didn't change the roll."

"If you keep talkin' crazy, I'm gonna have my doubts as to whether you can live on your own."

"I'd rather die than go to a nursing home," Earl huffed, crossing his arms. He meant it. He'd come to that conclusion after he'd spent three days in the hospital following a heart attack. That'd been five months ago, and it'd been the loneliest experience of his life. No visitors. Staff wouldn't let Brenda see him. "Family only." What family? Earl hadn't seen his kids in fifteen years and most of his friends had passed away.

"You're gonna die anyway from falling asleep while smoking—or forgetting to turn off the gas burner…just remember what I said about Betty."

****

Beatrice had been asleep in her queen-sized bed when she awoke to the clang of footfalls on the fire escape. She jerked the comforter aside, spilled out of bed and peered through the blinds. A pair of shapely legs, clad in pink spandex, floated by her third-floor window and up to the fourth-story fire escape.

Beatrice grabbed her mini baseball bat—a souvenir purchased at a New York Yankees game. She hobbled into the hallway, then paused at the landing before ascending the stairs. The cast impeded her from bombing her way to the fourth floor—it kept her rational.

Earl's room was off the kitchen. The door was ajar. The tube was on. Beatrice could hear booing and cheering from a live TV audience, punctuated by bleeps as talk show actors let off a string of F bombs. Earl loved his Jerry Springer reruns.

Beatrice heard other things as she approached the door. "Ooh, Earl. Ooh, Earl. You handsome devil. Move your hips when making that thrust!"

"Gotta take it easy, Baby. I been forgetting to take my Ginseng. Also, last time I tried this position, I pulled a muscle in my...."

Beatrice peered through the crack. Earl and Betty—or whatever the hell her name was—were fully clothed. They were playing a game of Tic Tac Throw. Earl's slippered feet were spread apart. Bent slightly at the waist, he squinted in concentration as he lobbed a polka-dotted bean bag at one of the squares, then moaned in ecstasy as the square spun on its pin to reveal the third X in a row.

XXX

"Score!" He punched the air.

"Ooh, Earl!!! You bad boy!" Brenda squealed, her big red hair gleaming from the glow of the TV. Her ample breasts bouncing inside her tight tank top.

Beatrice crept away from the door, the bat limp at her side. She would be sure to tell Earl to give Betty—Brenda—a spare key to the front door. She would let him know that Brenda was welcome to drop by any time—just not in pink spandex.

Winner of the Michael Doherty Award in Poetry, Amy Laprade's work has appeared in Silkworm, Write Angles Journal, Meat for Tea: the Valley Review and Canyon Voices, among others.

For more
information about this author,
visit www.amylaprade.com.

www.ingramcontent.com/pod-product-compliance
Lightning Source LLC
Chambersburg PA
CBHW051703090426
42736CB00013B/2514